First published in 2025 by Rock Point, an imprint of The Quarto Group,
142 West 36th Street, 4th Floor, New York, NY 10018, USA
(212) 779-4972 www.Quarto.com

10 9 8 7 6 5 4 3 2 1

ISBN: 978-1-57715-502-7

Digital edition published in 2025
eISBN: 978-0-7603-9405-2

Library of Congress Control Number:
2024949136

Group Publisher: Rage Kindelsperger
Editorial Director: Erin Canning
Creative Director: Laura Drew
Managing Editor: Cara Donaldson
Editor: Nicole James
Text: Sara Weiss
Cover and Interior Illustrations: Marieke Nelissen
Cover and Interior Design: Evelin Kasikov

Printed in China

A GOLDEN LIFE

What to Know and Love about the Golden Retriever

Sara Weiss

ROCK POINT

Dedication

To Mom and Dad

Introduction

The golden retriever is one of America's most popular dog breeds, ranking in the top ten on the American Kennel Club's (AKC) breed popularity charts since 1976. Goldens have portrayed iconic American family dogs in movies from *Homeward Bound* to *Marley and Me* to *Air Bud*, while in real life they work hard as sporting dogs, provide essential services to people with disabilities, and patiently tolerate the attention of sticky-handed toddlers. Reliable, loyal, friendly, empathetic, playful, funny, and beautiful inside and out, golden retrievers are the perfect pets and companions, bringing love and joy to everyone they meet!

A bit of the history of the breed: The golden retriever was first bred in the highlands of Scotland at Guisachan House, home of Sir Dudley Marjoribanks, later to become Baron Tweedmouth—I promise I'm not making these names up. He set out to create what he perceived as the ultimate breed of retriever, one that could withstand the climate and terrain of Scotland to fetch game for hunting. In 1865, he purchased Nous, a flat-coated retriever and the only yellow dog in a litter of black puppies. In 1868, Nous was mated with Belle, a Tweed water spaniel (a breed that is now extinct).

Who was this Nous character? For decades, people believed that Tweedmouth had purchased the dog from a trainer and that he was a Russian circus dog. Although it's fun to imagine your golden's ancestor performing tightrope tricks, unfortunately, this theory was disputed in the 1950s, when evidence surfaced that he had been purchased from a cobbler near the town of Brighton, in southern England.

As for the mom of the litter, Belle was a Tweed water spaniel who was described as "liver-colored." The breed came from the River Tweed area near the border of Scotland; it was a cross between the St. John's water dog and the regional water spaniel of the Northumberland and Borders coast.

All golden retrievers descend from the litter of pups that came from the mating of Nous and Belle.

The first of the litter's puppies were named Cowslip, Crocus, and Primrose. The yellow puppies from subsequent litters were further bred to create a new line. With contributions from wavy flat-coated retrievers, a red Irish setter, and more, the descendants of Nous and Belle eventually exhibited all the characteristics of today's goldens. Golden retrievers appeared in dog shows beginning in 1906, and the breed was officially recognized by the AKC in 1932.

Today, golden retrievers have medium-length hair and double coats. They come in varying shades of golden from almost yellow to a dark bronze. They are generally 21 to 24 inches (53–61 cm) tall, weigh 55 to 75 pounds (25–34 kg), and live for an average of 10 to 12 years. They have lustrous golden hair, a broad head, friendly and expressive eyes, a feathery tail, and a sturdy, muscular frame.

These sporting dogs were initially bred to retrieve waterfowl, but in the hundred years since, they have come to be our best companions, providing love, care, and protection. They are intelligent and easy to train, eager to please, affectionate, gentle, playful, boisterous, and trustworthy. These qualities make goldens brave and dependable service, therapy, and guide dogs as well.

For example, consider the story of Kelly and Beatrice, two golden retrievers from Italy. When Kelly was two years old and Beatrice was five, the two dogs swam out to sea to rescue a group of five boys at Forte dei Marmi beach in Tuscany. Swept out to sea by rip currents, the boys were about 160 feet (49 m) from shore and calling for help. Without hesitation, Kelly and Beatrice jumped into action, along with their handlers and the lifeguard on duty, to bring the boys safely back to shore. This is just one of the countless stories of these truly inspiring dogs.

Although they are widely beloved, goldens may not always be the right pet for every situation. If you are considering bringing a golden retriever into your home, you should learn as much as you can to ensure this unique breed is the right dog for you. They require a great deal of mental stimulation and exercise to stay happy, healthy, and engaged. They go through a cycle of shedding, known as "blowing their coats," as the seasons change, so expect to find tumbleweeds of golden fur rolling around. They are prone to health issues such as elbow and hip dysplasia, certain eye conditions, heart diseases, and cancer. Breeders should carefully screen for these conditions. You'll want to feed them a high-quality, age-appropriate diet, make sure to get them plenty of exercise, take them to the vet for regular visits, and of course, give them all the love. With routine health checks and lots of care, golden retrievers can live a lifetime of happiness.

When it comes down to it, goldens are some of the sweetest, kindest, friendliest, most lovable buds. They want to be with the ones they adore, to show affection and care, to play, and to retrieve. They are our fuzzy foot warmers, kid lovers, swimmers, best friends, protectors, and snuggle muffins–they are our goldens.

Joyous & Playful

Golden retrievers are **golden rays of sunshine!** They are a glass half full kind of pup—full of **optimistic energy** and **spirit** that's sure to rub off on everyone around them. That's the fabulous thing about dogs, isn't it? Their silly, playful, **happy energy** makes us smile. Whether our goldens are waiting with a goofy grin for us to throw that ball, clumsily knocking down everything in their path, or greeting us with a wet, slobbery kiss, they have a knack for lightening the mood.

Glass Half Full

Whereas some breeds can be a little moodier and more temperamental, golden retrievers are known for their chilled out, positive outlook. Some dogs might come to see the vet's office, for example, as an evil place based on past experiences (such as the times they got their ears flushed out or their anal glands expressed), but golden retrievers like to look at the bright side. First of all, the waiting room is a party–it's full of people and pets ready to say hello. And when you get through the hard stuff, there is a small chance you'll be offered a spoonful of canned spray cheese to lick.

Clumsy Clowns

Golden retrievers don't mean any harm, but they might accidentally step on a few toes from time to time. They can be a little bit clumsy, which really just adds to their charm and charisma. Of course, this is especially true when they are still puppies. In their extreme excitement, they'll dart around like a furry pinball, knocking into doors and walls, and that dust wiper of a tail will knock down anything in its way as if it has a mind of its own. So, golden retriever owners, you might want to clear those glass knickknacks and antique vases from your coffee table–and keep your little kiddos out of your golden's path when they get the zoomies. (Patience! They do tend to grow out of some of this over time.)

Loudest Bark

The Guinness World Record for loudest bark went to a six-year-old golden retriever named Charlie in 2012, and his record still stands! Charlie set the record at a national competition during the Purina Bark in the Park event in Adelaide, Australia. His bark measured in at 113.1 decibels, which is louder than a jet taking off and as loud as a steel mill! According to Charlie's owner, Belinda Freebairn, he developed his deep, booming bark when he was a year old. He was trained to bark only on command, so the noise wasn't a major annoyance in their neighborhood. Charlie smashed the previous record, held by a German shepherd from London who had a bark sounding off at 108 decibels. Way to go, Charlie! When you've got something to say, say it loud.

Forever Young

Although goldens can be intuitive, sensitive, and gentle, they can also be quite the goofballs–young at heart forevermore. These gentle giants don't always have an accurate sense of their own size. They tend to think they are actually lap dogs and will climb up onto you for a lick and a snuggle. They are also playful pups even in their old age. They are always ready to run around outside with a woobie in their mouth. They love to fetch, romp, and wrestle. They bound through life, bringing joy and companionship to all. Their playful nature inspires us to be more active and lead a healthier life too. Thank goodness for goldens!

Exercise from Puppyhood to Adulthood

A golden puppy should receive at least five minutes of exercise for every month they've been alive up until the age of one. (That's fifteen minutes of exercise a day for a three-month-old, twenty minutes for a four-month-old, and so on.) When they are still little and growing, you'll want to start slow and make sure not to overdo it to prevent injuries or bone and joint problems later on. But a little bit of exercise is necessary for their health, to strengthen your bond with your puppy, and to prevent them from engaging in destructive behaviors such as chewing, excessive barking, and aggression.

Adult and senior golden retrievers also need a lot of physical exercise–at least twenty to thirty minutes twice a day, and maybe up to two hours a day for a healthy, active doggy. Take your golden outside to hike, dock dive, or play fetch in the lake. Bring your dog along with you for walks or runs; just make sure to clear activities with your vet to ensure you are doing what's best for your furry friend. And watch out for signs of fatigue or soreness, especially as your dog gets older. Goldens will often push through pain because they love to play and be with you.

Grooming & Shedding

Golden retrievers are **gorgeous creatures.** They turn heads with their golden tresses, intelligent eyes, and steady gait. And their fur is their **signature feature.** They have the kind of fur everyone wants, the Jennifer-Aniston-of-the-'90s hairstyle of the dog world. Those golden waves! That long silky overcoat and soft, fuzzy undercoat!

Yes, they do shed just a little bit. Okay, let's be honest, they shed *a lot*. But think of all you could do with those golden fluff balls lying around! You could **knit a sweater or two,** maybe even a throw blanket. You could build a nest out of fur or fill a few pillows. (Sounds ridiculous, right? But some people really do this!)

There's a lot to learn about your golden retriever's gorgeous locks.

Double Coats

Golden retrievers—like other breeds such as Labradors, chow chows, and German shepherds—get to strut around with not one but *two* coats. There's a long, smooth outer coat that is waterproof and a soft, fuzzy undercoat that keeps them warm, protects them from the sun, and keeps them dry. They also have some long-feathered hairs that are wavy and lighten with age from golden to a cream color. Jealous?

Shedding Season

Ah, it's shedding season again. Hang your shedding decorations and prepare a special feast. This phenomenon takes place twice a year. As autumn turns the leaves from yellow and orange to brown, our golden pups drop their summer coats and thicken their winter fur. As springtime approaches and crocuses emerge from the earth, they shed this winter coat to stay cool in the coming months. This is also called "blowing their coats."

Throughout each shedding season, your home will be adorned with plenty of fur–fur in all nooks and crannies, fur where you least expect it. You'll find golden fur on your rugs, couches, and chairs, and you'll see tumbleweeds of fur that roll when the wind blows. When you try to clean up the long fur, it will clog the vacuum, coil around the brushes, and get stuck in the tubes. But that's a small price to pay for the beauty of a golden.

Fur to Fashion

You won't be able to hide the fact that you live with a golden when you're out in public because there will be fur on all of your clothes, even stuck to your socks when you take your shoes off and on your butt (which the people behind you in yoga class will appreciate). Although this fur phenomenon will settle down a little bit after shedding season has come to a close, don't worry–you'll be able to enjoy the fun year-round as well. Golden retrievers still shed a moderate amount all the time.

Dog Yarn

Don't waste that precious dog fur when you could be spinning it into yarn and knitting sweaters. Believe it or not, dog wool is actually a thing! The official term for this kind of wool is chiengora—that's chien, or "dog" in French, combined with gora from angora.

It may not be common today, but spinning dog hair is nothing new. It has roots going back to prehistoric Scandinavia and to the histories of various Native American cultures, including the Navajo Nation in the Southwest. The Coast Salish people in British Columbia bred a small white woolly dog, now extinct, whose fur they wove into both decorative and practical blankets.

Chiengora is actually even warmer than sheep's wool, and it's a breathable and sustainable textile. Not all dog fur can be used for wool, though. The fur needs to be from those breeds with an undercoat of long hair such as golden retrievers, chow chows, or Newfoundlands. Sometimes the yarn must also be combined with other fibers such as sheep or alpaca wool. So, yes, goldens are shedders, but why not make the most of a hairy situation?

Glow-Up

You can find a lot of goodies hiding in that luscious mane–mud, bugs, burrs, thorns, or snow, for example. If your kid is missing a LEGO or you can't seem to find your favorite earring, it's not a bad idea to search the fluff.

To maintain your golden's double coat, you might need to visit the groomer quite a lot. They will brush, bathe, and dry your golden, clean their ears, check for infection, cut their nails, brush their teeth, and generally give them a pretty awesome glow-up.

If you are doing it yourself, you'll want to brush through your golden's fur with a grooming rake at least once a week (and probably more like every day during peak shedding) to prevent matting and to get rid of excess fur. Pay particular attention to the base of your goldie's ears, their haunches, and under their tail. Their undercoat will shed itself seasonally, but if you want to help it along, you can give your golden a blow out. You'll probably want to be outside when you do this, and you might want to situate yourself away from the wind–unless golden-fur-in-the-face is the look you're going for.

Shed Defender

If the tumbleweeds of golden fur rolling around your house are getting to you, there are solutions on the market. Consider looking into de-shedding gloves, special tools and brushes, robot vacuums, and special shampoos. You can buy couches that are dog hair–proof and special liners for your car seats. There's also an item called The Shed Defender. The Walter brothers, Tyler and Myles, appeared on *Shark Tank* in 2018 to pitch this garment. It looks kind of like a onesie or leotard for your dog, and it is designed to trap the dog hair and keep your home, car, and clothes free from pet fur. Meant to provide a snug fit that can help calm anxious dogs, the Shed Defender can also cover hot spots and replace the traditional post-surgery "cone of shame."

Guisachan Gathering

Every five years, hundreds of golden retrievers return to their ancestral home in the Scottish Highlands for a reunion. They pose for photographs in front of the ruins of the old mansion that used to belong to Baron Tweedmouth, founder of the breed. The 2023 photograph shows nearly five hundred goldens in a grassy field in front of the ruins, clouds rolling in behind them.

Hosted by the Golden Retriever Club of Scotland, the Guisachan Gathering draws golden enthusiasts from around the world including Ireland, Germany, Switzerland, the Czech Republic, the United States, Australia, Canada, and Croatia. The Club is comprised of members who have the well-being of all golden retrievers at heart, and it promotes responsible breeding and ownership.

Participants at the gathering can take part in events such as hunting dog demonstrations, a dog show, and a haggis hurling competition (for humans.) You can also take a photograph in front of a brass statue of a golden retriever that was erected in Tomich village in 2014.

Scottish Gun Dogs

Golden retrievers were originally bred by the elite to retrieve waterfowl for hours on end in the mountains and glens of Scotland, a cold and wet terrain. Until then, there was not a dog as successful at retrieving birds from both water and land while also serving as a hunter's companion with a **gentle** and **friendly demeanor.** They have an incredible sense of smell, and they are eager to please, which makes them easy to train. Their **intelligence, energy level,** and **stamina** make them ideal hunting companions. Although many of us are not looking to go hunting with our pups, the drive to fetch and retrieve is still in their DNA. They are **active, outdoorsy, adventure-loving** dogs. They need a lot of exercise to stay happy and relaxed and to be their best selves.

Retrievers

Because they were bred to retrieve, you might find them bringing you unexpected items: a dead mouse, a crumpled and chewed-up water bill, a week-old apple slice, the toilet brush. . . . They will drop the item at your feet and stand there proudly with their head held high, tail wagging, awaiting your praise.

Because of their natural instincts, they are also masters at playing fetch. They can be a bit clumsy sometimes, though, and they might barrel through any obstacles in their way, such as fences, cones, or trees, so make sure the coast is clear before hurling that ball.

Swimmers

A golden retriever's happy place is in the water. They will find the nearest puddle, lake, sprinkler, or kiddie pool and splash around. They were bred to race into the near-frozen waters of Scotland to retrieve duck or waterfowl, so diving into the water is in their DNA. Just be ready for a wet and muddy dog to return to you–and when they shake, they'll soak the whole family.

Golden owners will tell you their pups can swim for ages as long as their ball keeps getting tossed in the water. They could swim to exhaustion. Some say they have never seen the limit; their golden could swim forever. That doesn't mean they *should*, though. Michele Godlevski, NADD Dock Diving Judge, recommends ten-minute active swim sessions to avoid exhaustion or water toxicity. She also says using a doggy life vest can provide extra support. (She doesn't say this, but I'd like to add that it can also make your golden look like a J.Crew model, especially when they are standing on a boat staring off into the distance.)

Divers

Golden retrievers also can dive underwater and retrieve objects, thanks to their natural abilities and the fascinating mammalian diving response. The mammalian diving response is a reflex that is triggered by cold water; it causes a reduced heart rate and redirects blood flow to vital organs such as the heart and brain. It helps dogs—as well as many other mammals—manage submersion in cold water by conserving oxygen and protecting vital organs, supporting their survival in such conditions. (Interesting fact: Some human babies have the mammalian diving response up until six months old!) Although goldens might be able to hold their breath and dive 15 feet (4.6 m) below the surface, frequent diving might lead to water entering their nose and mouth, which can cause respiratory issues. Make sure your dog doesn't overdo it, and monitor them closely to prevent potential health problems related to underwater diving.

Movers

Golden retrievers *need* to run around and expend energy. In fact, it's recommended that adults get up to two hours of exercise a day! And although goldies are known for being easygoing and laid-back, they can become hyperactive or destructive if their exercise needs are not met. Exercise helps their hearts and their minds, reducing stress and anxiety. Exercise also fills their cup, giving them time to bond with you and be social, which is something they love to do. You might take them hiking with you, go for a run or walk, play tug of war or fetch, go dock diving, or take them to the dog park.

You might also sign your dog up for agility training when they are fully grown. Agility training involves a preset obstacle course that your dog will learn to navigate, challenging their fitness and engaging them mentally as they learn new skills such as running up ramps, launching over hurdles, and barreling through tunnels. Exercise can bring physical benefits, and walking your golden retriever with other dogs can help them gain confidence and comfort around other animals and people. It can also help you build your confidence as a dog handler.

Diving Dogs

Golden retrievers can be masters at chasing balls and often aren't afraid to get wet. If you've got a golden that fits this profile, you might want to investigate a sport called Diving Dogs or Dock Divers.

In this sport, you throw a toy into a pool while your dog waits on one end of a 40-foot (12 m) dock. On your command, your dog sprints along the dock and jumps to retrieve it. Starting divers might jump as little as 2 feet (0.6 m), with more advanced pups going as far as 30 feet (9 m) or more. Titles earned through North America Diving Dogs (NADD) association are recognized by the AKC.

The three main disciplines of dock diving are:

- Big Air, a long jump for dogs. The distance is judged from the end of the dock to where the "tail set" breaks the water.
- Extreme Vertical, a high jump for dogs.
- Speed Retrieve, which is a timed event. A toy is suspended above the water and, on command, the dog jumps to release it.

Dock diving is hosted by local clubs around the United States. There are also national events and a world championship. Find a club or event in your area!

Soft Mouths

A hunter needs a steady dog who will sit still and retrieve only when called on. The best hunting dogs also need to have a soft mouth, or the ability to retrieve a bird and carry it back gently and without damaging it. Golden retrievers have been bred to have soft mouths, which not only makes them ideal hunting dogs, but also means they have a strong bite inhibition, making them the perfect family-friendly pups.

Soft-mouthed dogs can, apparently, carry raw eggs in their mouths without cracking the shell. If you're looking for a helper who can hand you the ingredients for a breakfast frittata, your sous chef might be lying at your feet right now. (Also, your golden would look quite cute in a chef's hat–something to consider!)

Tennis Ball Hoarder

Picture a golden retriever smiling at you with those soft brown eyes and a mouth full of tennis balls. A golden retriever named Finley holds the Guinness World Record for holding the most tennis balls in his mouth at one time. Finley, who lives with the Molloy family in Canandaigua, New York, started carrying four tennis balls in his mouth when he was two years old. Gradually, the number of tennis balls increased to six.

"My dad would throw him a tennis ball," Finley's owner Erin said. "He'd catch it, drop it, then wait for my dad to throw another. Rather than bringing just one ball back to my dad, he brought back all six! He's been a ball hoarder for quite some time now."

The previous record belonged to another golden retriever, Augie, who held five tennis balls in 2003.

Finley celebrated his award at a “pawty” with his neighbors, enjoying a tennis ball doggy treat atop a cake with his name on it. When he’s not breaking records, Finley loves to swim, play fetch, roll on his back in the snow, and run after critters in the garden.

Runners-up

Golden retrievers are **incredibly popular, charming,** and **likable;** we all know that. Yet sometimes, it feels like they are trying to live up to those other retrievers. You know the ones I'm talking about. They were number one in popularity in the United States for thirty-one years . . . they are also really into water and catching wild fowl . . . their name starts with an L and ends with an R. . . . That's right, Labrador retrievers have topped the popularity charts for years. (Until the clownish little French bulldogs came along in 2022 to dethrone them. That's for another day.) Golden retrievers are **amazing in their own right** and should never feel like second best—like they are always the bridesmaid, never the bride. The truth is that they don't care much about the charts. But if they did care, they might wonder, "What on Earth does the Labrador have that I don't?"

Outward Confidence

Although both golden retrievers and Labradors are considered personable, empathetic, and friendly, goldens can be less outwardly confident than Labradors. They might be a little bit more reserved and sensitive. At a party, goldens might be the ones to hold back a little bit to assess the situation whereas Labradors would get in there and start sniffing all the guests. Labradors are slightly more exuberant and outgoing, while golden retrievers can be gentler and calmer. This might give Labradors the tiniest edge when it comes to trainability as service dogs because Labradors show no hesitancy in approaching strangers when their owner needs assistance. But goldens also make for fabulous service dogs for a number of reasons. They are generally outgoing as well, alert, intelligent, loyal, sociable, eager to please, naturally sensitive to people and their emotions, and nonaggressive. Instead of a weakness, their relatively calm and gentle demeanor is one of the qualities golden owners find so appealing.

Hair Length

We've already talked about one of the great joys of owning a golden retriever–the golden furballs you'll find tucked into every crevice of your home. Well, Labs shed a lot too! Both breeds have double coats and both shed like crazy to prepare for warmer or cooler seasons.

A golden retriever's hair happens to be longer than a Lab's coat. We all know this. It's their signature feature! Maybe if you were comparing the two breeds side by side, you could say that a golden's fur creates *more* of a mess than a Lab's. It might take a little bit longer for a golden's fur to dry and their mane might hold onto slightly more mud and debris than a Lab's–but a golden retriever's wavy coat is classic, lustrous, luscious, beautiful, and so so so soft! So there!

Also, do you think you could spin a skein of wool out of your Labrador's fur? Not so easy, huh? When it comes to knitting sweaters out of your dog's tresses, golden retrievers for the win!

Best in Show, or No?

With their reputation as a fan favorite, you'd think golden retrievers would be killing it at the Westminster Kennel Club Dog Show, strutting around town with a heap of medals dangling from their necks. But no–in fact, a golden retriever has never won Best in Show. (Gasp!) Sure, they've had their moments, placing five times in their group since they began competing at Westminster in 1928 and winning Best of Group once in 2006. Daniel the golden retriever even won the Sporting Group at the 2020 Westminster Dog Show. But despite their many attempts and close calls, goldens have yet to walk away with the whole title.

Christine Miele, the Eastern Vice President of the Golden Retriever Club of America, is not losing sleep over this dilemma. "If you had a popularity contest, we would win," she told *The New York Times*. "We have everything in the world going for us except Westminster, and I think we're okay with that."

And going back to the friendly rivalry, Labradors are in the same boat. When it comes to Best in Show, Labs and goldens are 0 and 0.

Colors of the Rainbow

Perhaps Labradors gain a slight edge because they come in a variety of colors–yellow, black, and chocolate–whereas goldens are only one color, golden. However, that golden luster comes in many shades, from dark to light, from cream to fox red. Goldens can be light golden like the morning sun. They can be a warm, classic golden; a rich, dark golden with hues of amber; or even a lustrous coppery tone. When they are puppies, their coats are often light, almost white. As they grow, their coats start to thicken and the shades will change. Goldens of many shades and hues can make their way into the show ring, because the AKC recognizes golden, darkish gold, and gentle gold.

The truth is, both breeds are absolutely beloved and adored for all of their fabulous traits. Who's competing anyway?

The Canadian, English, and American

Keep in mind, as we're comparing the two breeds, that not all goldens are the same. There are some subtle differences between the three main varieties of goldens—English, Canadian, and American—and it has nothing to do with their choice of black pudding, maple syrup, or apple pie. Canadian goldens have a slightly thinner coat than the others, and they are usually taller and leaner than English golden retrievers. English goldens are a bit stockier than their North American mates, they have wider heads and squarer noses, and their fur tends to be a little bit lighter. American golden retrievers are generally lankier than their British counterparts. Let's celebrate these differences! It's a part of who they are.

Celebs and Their Golden Pals

A number of dog-loving celebrities pride themselves on owning golden retrievers.

Jennifer Garner's golden retriever, Birdie, has recently been promoted to work as a service dog, visiting patients at the Children's Hospital Los Angeles to offer support. Garner and her pup tried the "hands in" or "paws in challenge," a social media challenge in which pet owners put their hands in front of their pet to see if they would respond. To Garner's delight, Birdie responded by putting her paw in on the first try.

The WNBA basketball player Caitlin Clark loves her pup, a golden retriever named Bella. Before the first day of her sophomore year at Iowa, Caitlin and Bella sat posed for a picture with "First Day of School" signs. Caitlin's major: business. Bella's major: napping. Caitlin's hobby: Candy Crush. Bella's hobby: walking. Caitlin wrote, "I am 6 ft. 0 in. tall," and for Bella, "I am 2 ft. 0 in." Clark also owns a life-sized cardboard cutout of Bella that her family brought to sit in the stands next to them for some of her NCAA games.

The late Betty White, the OG Golden Girl, owned golden retrievers all her life and was a spokesperson for the Morris Animal Foundation, helping to find a cure for canine diseases. She also starred in a 2001 film called *The Retrievers*, which is about a golden retriever who goes on a mission to recover her lost puppies. Some people have been known to name their goldens after the stars of *The Golden Girls*—kinda cute!

All-American Family Dogs

Although goldens originally hailed from the United Kingdom, they've come to represent the quintessential white-picket-fence American dog. It's because of their reputation for being **gentle, kind,** and **good with kids.** They have also graced our television screens in a number of shows and movies. They have resided in the **White House,** and one golden even became mayor of an American town!

Dogs on the Screen

Golden retrievers excel in the spotlight: *The Art of Racing in the Rain*, the Lindsay Lohan version of *The Parent Trap*, *Homeward Bound*, *A Dog's Purpose*, *You've Got Mail*, *Hawkeye*, *Full House*, and more.

Buddy, one of the most famous golden actors, starred in the 1997 Disney film *Air Bud* and had quite an acting career. In 1989, Buddy's life changed drastically after he was a stray dog taken in by Kevin DiCicco and brought home to San Diego, California. DiCicco trained Buddy to play basketball, baseball, football, soccer, and hockey. Buddy started to get famous, appearing on *America's Funniest Home Videos* and later on David Letterman.

Finally, Buddy was cast in *Air Bud*, in which he played a basketball-playing golden retriever. Although the director admits it took quite a few tries to capture the winning shots, that really is Buddy doing his own tricks in the film–jumping up on his hind legs as the ball is tossed to him and using his body and mouth to fling the ball up and into the hoop. He shoots, he scores!

Presidential Dogs

Golden retrievers are no strangers to the White House. President Ford had a golden retriever named Liberty while in office, and President Reagan owned a golden named Victory. In his 1979 memoir *A Time to Heal*, Ford wrote about how Victory became part of their family. In an effort to surprise the president and his wife, Ford's photographer, David Hume Kennerly, called a kennel owner to inquire about adopting a golden retriever. The kennel owner wanted to be sure the dog was going to a good home and asked various questions such as, "Do they own or rent?"

David thought for a minute. "I guess you might call it public housing," he said.

Ford was indeed surprised when a copper-colored puppy showed up in the Oval Office one day.

Goldie Palooza

Imagine nearly 1,000 golden retrievers hanging out together in a sunny field with music playing in the background—sort of like Woodstock for dogs (minus some of the things that, you know, took place at Woodstock).

Goldie Palooza began when a family in the South Bay area of California organized a weekend meet-up with their pup Hugo Maxwell and friends in the golden retriever community they'd met on social media. The day was a huge success. It featured activities such as beach play, walks, pool time, hikes, road trips, and kayaking. A year later, to celebrate the anniversary of this meet-up, the group put together a volunteer-run festival they named Goldie Palooza, and all proceeds of the event benefitted golden retriever rescues.

There were 350 golden retrievers at the first Goldie Palooza, which took place in the fall of 2017 in Huntington Beach, California. Every year, the numbers go up: 681 goldens in 2018 (at a beautiful private property in Silverado, California), 751 goldens in 2022, and 936 goldens in 2023!

Mayor Max

One golden retriever has even held political office, winning a mayoral election in the town of Idyllwild, California, in 2012. Idyllwild, an unincorporated town, had previously had no mayors or politicians (human or otherwise). A nonprofit organization, Idyllwild Animal Rescue Friends (ARF), held an election as a fundraiser and residents were allowed to nominate their dogs or cats. With fourteen dogs and two cats in the running, a golden named Max dominated the field with a whopping two-thirds of the votes to become Idyllwild's first mayor ever. He had a small staff consisting of Chiefs of Staff (and owners) Phyllis and Glenn.

Sadly, Mayor Max passed away in the middle of his term. He was succeeded by Maximus Mighty-Dog Mueller II as well as two deputy mayors–Mikey and Mitzi (Mikey Mighty-Dog Mueller and Mitzi Mighty-Dog Mueller)–all related by blood.

While in office, Mayor Max I made invaluable contributions to his town. He showed up at weddings, hospitals, birthday parties, nursing homes, and charity events. He became a local celebrity, too, with his face appearing on billboards and merch for the town–a face that brought a smile to everyone else's faces.

American Trailblazer

Perhaps the very first golden retriever to walk on American soil was a nine-year-old pup named Sol, who accompanied the founder of the breed's son, Archie Marjoribanks, to Texas. Sol lived there with Archie on Rocking Horse Ranch along with the family's prized Angus Aberdeen cattle.

Lord Tweedmouth's 1868 litter from Nous and Belle created the three yellow puppies Crocus, Primrose, and Cowslip, the very first golden retrievers. Cowslip sired a new branch of the family tree, to which Sol was born just a few generations later. The prized pups of these earliest generations were often kept in the family and were only gifted with care to family and friends, who would value them as the ultimate gentleman's hunting dog.

Archie Marjoribanks and Sol lived on the family cattle ranch between 1891 and 1894. There is a black and white photograph of Archie sitting beside his handsome dog in the historical records of early ancestors of the breed.

It's a Wonderful Life

So many of us know what it feels like to love and cherish our dogs, and we also have to experience the heartache of having to let them go. Pups make their way into our hearts. If you're reading this book, that's probably true for you, and it's just as true for the rich and famous, including legendary actor James "Jimmy" Stewart, the star of *It's a Wonderful Life* and other classics. Back in 1981, Jimmy Stewart spoke about his special bond with his golden retriever, Beau, when he appeared on *The Tonight Show with Johnny Carson*. He read a poem about his furry friend, "I'll Never Forget a Dog Named Beau."

When he was done, the host of the show, Johnny Carson, wiped his eyes. It's clear from the warm wave of applause that Stewart touched the hearts of everyone in the audience as well. You can find the video on YouTube if you feel like having a sniffle.

Superheroes

Golden retrievers make for reliable service animals and can be trained to perform different tasks to help people with mental and physical disabilities. They have what it takes to provide care that can change a person's life, including a **protective nature, a quiet confidence,** and **a zest for life.** They are eager to please, calm, friendly, trusting, loyal, intelligent, and easily adaptable. As medium-sized dogs, they have the strength and height to open doors, push buttons, and use their frame to support their owner.

Goldens can help people with mobility, pull a wheelchair, or support someone with balance issues. They can work as psychiatric dogs by calming anxiety attacks, fetching medicine, alerting people when they sense a seizure coming on, and even providing Deep Pressure Therapy (DPT). They can also work as guide dogs, helping people with visual impairments navigate their surroundings. They have the size and stamina to **work hard all day** and are **smart** enough to pick up on training quickly, but perhaps their most remarkable trait is that they are **emotionally intelligent** enough to sense when people need their help.

Orca

A UK golden retriever named Orca was trained as an assistance dog and paired with Cheryl Alexander in 2003. Cheryl suffers from a neurological condition that prevents her from walking, and she uses a wheelchair to get around. Orca learned more than 150 commands and was trained to help Cheryl with everyday tasks.

One day, Cheryl lost control of her wheelchair and fell off an embankment into a drainage ditch below, her 300-pound (136 kg) wheelchair pinning her in the water.

"Get help!" she shouted. Orca took off and, after a long while, returned wet from the rain without his collar and with his service jacket pulled down. Later, it was determined that Orca had chased down a passerby and tried to alert him, but the man assumed Orca was a stray and held his collar to lead him away. Orca slid free from his collar to break away—a decision that went against his training but showed how determined he was.

"Get help!" Cheryl shouted again. Orca ran for more than a mile (1.6 km) in the rain looking for help and finally found a jogger who turned out to be one of Cheryl's neighbors. When they found her, she had hypothermia and was drifting in and out of consciousness. The rescue team asserted that Orca had absolutely saved Cheryl's life.

Sampson

An extraordinary golden retriever, Sampson, was paired with owner Joey Ramp. Joey suffered a brain injury and PTSD after a life-altering accident that had left her with mobility issues and nerve damage. Sampson was trained to alert Joey when he sensed that she was having panic and anxiety symptoms. He helped her climb stairs, supported her balance when necessary, and retrieved items for her.

After Joey received her PhD in neuroscience from the University of Illinois, she knew she would need Sampson's assistance in the lab to support her, as he always did, so she could work to her full potential. At that time, however, service dogs weren't allowed in the lab. Joey and Sampson fought to change the university's policy, and Sampson became the first service dog who was granted access to a molecular and cellular biology laboratory and a genetics laboratory. Picture an adorable golden in goggles, a custom white lab coat, and booties–best lab partner ever!

NFL Dog

A golden retriever named Ben has become a fan favorite football mascot. Ben's owner, Kirk Herbstreit, is always busy announcing games; he works as an analyst on Amazon Prime Video's *Thursday Night Football*, as part of the crew for ESPN's *GameDay*, and an announcer for Saturday night college football games on ESPN and ABC. And he likes to bring his trusty ten-year-old, 95-pound (43 kg) golden pal into the booth with him to keep him company and boost team morale.

Herbstreit says their personalities perfectly complement each other. They are both calm and analytical. "It's his personality that makes me appreciate who he is," Herbstreit said. "He's a partner. He's made a night-and-day difference for me being on the road."

Fans stop to say hello to Ben on the road, at the tailgate, or in the stadium. His popularity has soared with recent appearances in college and NFL games. Ben has been seen rolling on the grass near the 50-yard line while teams do their pregame warm-ups. He was also filmed getting pets from Aaron Rodgers and joining in sideline drills to warm up for the Browns vs. Jets game.

Surrogate Mama

A golden retriever named Kassy became a surrogate mother to three African painted puppies at the Potawatomi Zoo in Indiana. The Indiana Council for Animal Welfare connected the zoo with Kassy after the endangered African painted pups were abandoned by their parents. There are only 7,000 African painted dogs (also known as African wild dogs or African painted wolves) left in the world. The zoo's staff reached out to professionals who could help them determine how to help the pups, and the Indiana Council for Animal Welfare paired them with Kassy, a golden retriever who had just had a litter of her own. She and her puppies came to the zoo, and she nursed the surrogate pups along with her own. Go Mama Kassy!

Deer Rescue

A golden retriever named Storm showed extraordinary bravery by rescuing a fawn in distress off the shore of Long Island, New York. During a morning stroll, Storm noticed the young deer struggling in the water, battling the current. Without hesitation, he jumped in and pulled the fawn to safety. But Storm didn't stop at just rescuing the fawn—he stayed by its side, nuzzling and gently pawing the deer to help it regain its strength. Storm's owner, in awe of his pup's heroic act, managed to capture the moment on video. The fawn was promptly taken into the care of Strong Island Animal Rescue League, where it received the treatment it needed to recover.

Beauty & Brains

Golden retrievers have got it all—**beauty and brains.** (That's as well as **kindness, empathy, affability, a positive outlook,** and more.) The works! Oh, aren't they beautiful with their silky, shimmering, wavy golden coat, their kind eyes, their velvety ears, and their **endearing smile?** And they are ranked fourth among dog breeds in intelligence because of their natural instincts, adaptive smarts, and strong work ethic. These canines are no joke. No wonder they are so popular.

Beauty

According to the official AKC standards for the golden retriever's general appearance, they should be a symmetrical, powerful, active dog with kind and intelligent eyes, an eager personality, and a well-balanced body. They should move with a smooth and powerful gait, so that the feathery tail is carried, as breed fanciers say, with a "merry action."

So, you know, in short–they're pretty.

But the most beautiful things about goldens are the way their heart and kind spirit shine through their sweet gaze, the way their soft expression shows patience and care, and the way their golden fur warms your toes on a cold day. Their beauty on the outside reflects their beauty within.

Brains

Goldens are brainy too! There are many different ways to show smarts. According to research done by dog expert Stanley Coren, PhD, a dog's mental ability is close to that of a two- to two-and-a-half-year-old human. Smart dogs can learn new commands, understand an average of 165 words, solve complex problems, count to four or five, and dupe us to get treats. Out of all dog breeds, goldens rank fourth in intelligence, which means they are considered one of the smartest dog breeds out there. (Border collies are number one.)

Golden retrievers are smart when it comes to adaptive intelligence, or a dog's ability to learn from their environment to solve problems on their own. They are also super brainy when it comes to instinctive intelligence, which is how dogs can instinctively perform a task they were bred to do: herders herd, pointers point, guard dogs guard, and retrievers . . . retrieve. Goldens have also got what it takes when it comes to working and obedience intelligence, which is indicated by their incredible ability to learn from humans. They are highly trainable and can learn to complete tasks and respond to our language.

Teacup Goldens

What do you get when you breed golden retrievers with cocker spaniels (for smaller size) and poodles (for more manageable fur)? Breeders call them mini or teacup golden retrievers, a smaller version of the breed that is purported to shed less and have fewer health issues. They weigh 20 to 40 pounds (9 to 18 kg) and stand 14 to 18 inches (35 to 45 cm) tall. Other names for them include comfort retriever, mini goldens, and golden minis. Although the trend for miniature pups is taking off, attracting apartment dwellers looking for a compact companion and people looking for a more hypoallergenic dog, there is some dispute about the validity of the breed. Some golden owners warn potential teacup buyers that the breeding of these dogs may not be ethical, may not be consistent, and may not follow standard practices. (In fact, mini goldens are not recognized by the AKC.)

Although there's no doubt that these pint-sized cuties have got the look, buyers should research carefully and always be sure to find a reputable breeder.

One or the Other

We've talked about how trainable and intelligent goldens can be. Service dogs can retrieve medication, open doors, and even turn on lights for people with mobility issues. Sporty pups can take part in high-level agility training, where they navigate obstacle courses that test their speed, precision, and teamwork with their handler.

But for some lovable goofballs, their fetching good looks are greater than their smarts. This is the case for Hudson B. Mason, a.k.a. "The Goodest Golden Good Boy" (@HudsonBeGood). Online, you can find funny scenes of Hudson with captions such as "Beauty>Brains."

In one video, the caption reads, "98% beauty. 2% brains. 100% booty." Hudson poses at the beach, sitting pretty with a bandanna around his neck. Then he is startled by the ocean, he struggles to retrieve a tennis ball with a net in the way, he barks at a pair of sunglasses as if they're alive, and he lies with his paws on the bed and booty on the floor.

It's all in good fun. Hudson charms his viewers and his owners too. "Dog is my love language," his owner says.

Cute Effect

Why is it that our pups are just irresistible when they sit and stare at us with a slight tilt of the head? So much so that our resolve goes away and we find ourselves sprinkling some of the shredded cheese we were about to eat into their food bowls?

Alexander Varakin, a professor of psychology at Eastern Kentucky University, performed a study entitled, "With This Tilt I Dub Cute: Head Tilt Increases Cuteness in Puppies and Adult Dogs." His goal was to determine whether behavioral features can have an impact on cuteness as well as previously studied physical features. Varakin studied the effect that a head tilt has on a puppy's cuteness by showing participants photos of adult dogs and puppies with upright heads or tilted. The result? Participants found the dog with the tilted head to be significantly cuter. "These results suggest that head tilt, when controllable, can increase cuteness of animals that are already very cute (puppies) and those that are less cute (adult dogs)."

Good Vibes

Has anyone ever told you that you have **golden retriever energy?** Take it as a compliment! This means you are **super friendly, positive, upbeat,** and **pretty lovable** too. Golden retrievers are all good vibes. They're the kind of friend you always want to have around. You know they'll shine some of their bright light on you whenever you're in their presence, and show you **kindness and empathy** when you need it most.

Comfort

Sometimes, the most sensitive souls make for the best companions. Anyone who has owned a golden retriever knows that they have the capacity to show real and true empathy to the humans in their lives. They can read the room, tune into their humans' moods and intentions, and adjust their behavior accordingly. They can intuit what kind of attention you might need, whether it's to be left alone, snuggle, play, or laugh. They seem to sense when you are blue. They'll climb on your lap and lay their head on your shoulder, run over and start licking your face, or lie at your feet to give you some solace and fuzzy warmth.

People Pleasers

Goldens very much want to please you, and they will pretty much do anything for you. Bred alongside hunters to bring them prey, goldens have a natural inclination to work with their humans and to offer them what they need. Keep that in mind when your golden stands before you with an offering in their mouth—a doggy toy, a remote, a ball of socks, or a football. It's a gift!

This eagerness to please makes goldens easy to train and well-suited to respond to commands, especially when positive reinforcements, such as treats and pets, are in it for them. We can work and play alongside one another, and together we can form an unbreakable bond.

Go with the Flow

Goldens are friendly and happy, but they are also chill and easygoing. That's a good combination, right? They're the one you call up when you're headed out for an adventure, going for a morning jog, looking forward to a lazy rainy stay-in-bed-and-snuggle kind of day, or in the mood to be social—golden retrievers are up for anything. They are versatile like that. Golden retrievers can be mellow and will go with the flow, which makes it easy to bring them along to a big family barbecue, a crowded street fair, or a friend's house. They'll say hello to the people they meet, lie down in the sun, thwap their tail in the grass, walk along with you wherever you're going, and happily receive the greetings and pets from strangers.

Golden Retriever Boyfriend (GRB)

A GRB is not afraid to show his emotions, has an insane amount of energy, is trusting and kind, can be naive, and is always positive. He is affectionate and loving, attached to his partner, and always seeking stimulation. When his partner is in distress, he will be their rock. He is also a goofball and a jokester, sometimes to a fault.

Now, what would our golden retrievers make of this comparison? Would they be honored? A little offended? Think it's all in good fun?

Mood Lifters

Wherever golden retrievers go, they make the vibes better. A wag of the tail or an affectionate greeting can improve the atmosphere in any setting.

This was the case for Julie Barton, author of *The New York Times* bestselling memoir *Dog Medicine: How My Dog Saved Me from Myself*. Her connection with her golden retriever, Bunker, saved her from her depression. She reflects on the power of dogs: "For me, just watching them–their lack of self-consciousness, their ability to find joy in the littlest things–it's still teaching me." Having a dog also helps her to get outside for walks, keep a regular schedule, and appreciate the small things.

Goldens have the power to make people feel valued and at ease. It seems like such a simple thing, but truly, these dogs can change someone's life just by being who they are.

Aloha Vibes

Some golden retrievers, such as Hobie the rescue dog, bring Aloha vibes to those around them. Hobie's life changed forever when he was rescued from the streets of East Los Angeles and taken to foster care. He was then connected to Chris De Aboitiz, an Australian dog whisperer, former world champion tandem surfer, and founder of SupDogOz, a holistic lifestyle brand that combines his passions for the ocean, dogs, and teaching.

Chris had come in from Australia to participate in the Surf City Surf Dog competition, which is pretty much exactly as it sounds: city dogs competing in a surfing competition (with humans on the board to guide them). Chris had taught dogs to surf before, but this time, he wanted to find a rescue dog who had never been in the water. He hoped to bring awareness to the incredible mission of rescue organizations and help these lovable dogs find good homes.

Training Hobie took time and patience. First, Chris helped Hobie get comfortable around water, and then taught him how to balance on a board and stay still. Hobie and Chris rode a few epic waves in the competition, earning Hobie a silver medal. And the best part: At the end of the competition, Hobie's new adoptive family was there watching and cheering him on, and they were ready to bring Hobie home and give him the good life he deserved.

A Happy?

You've probably heard of a flock of birds, a gaggle of geese, and a pride of lions. How about a murder of crows, a caravan of camels, or a troop of baboons? And what would you call a group of golden retrievers? The Golden Dog Farm in Cambridge, Vermont, refers to their pack of goldens as a "happy." If you want to visit the farm, you can take part in the Happy Hour Golden Retriever Experience, in which you'll get a chance to cuddle up with a "happy" of ten or more fluffy golden retriever pups while soaking up the natural beauty of the picturesque Green Mountains. Sounds pretty ideal, right? While you're there, you can also taste maple syrup and raw honey at the Worple family farm or enjoy a bee experience.

Love

If you have room in your heart for giving a golden retriever **a good life,** you will be rewarded with **adoration, affection,** and **love.** Their hearts are big, and they can offer kindness and sweetness when you need it most.

Warmth

Goldens can not only make you feel warm on the inside, they'll warm you on the outside too. They're like a fuzzy rug that follows you around wherever you go. And when you see them there–smiling at you, gazing at you with empathetic eyes, or resting their snouts on their graceful legs–it's impossible not to pet them and give them snuggles.

Gentle Giants

A golden's gentle, protective nature makes them lovable too. You might find your golden sitting in the middle of a crowd of kids, smiling that classic golden smile, head held high. They are happy to be part of the crew, but they also take their role as bodyguards seriously. They will look after the children, giving them kisses when they fall or alerting you when someone is hurt. They will endure a great deal of toddler rough play and remain patient. They are docile and gentle, and their presence gives us peace of mind.

Affection

Affection is when your golden follows you wherever you go, curls up by your feet, or leans against you just to be close. Affection is when they march over to you with a toy in their mouth and drop it at your feet. It's when they sit on your lap and lick your face to let you know they adore you. It's the greeting you get when you come home—or sometimes if you even just leave the room and come back—wild excitement, paws skittering on the floor, and fluffy tail swinging in circles as if they haven't seen you in years.

Loyalty

Although golden retrievers are friendly and outgoing with friends and strangers alike, they know who their people are. According to a *Reader's Digest* survey, they rank in the top four loyal dog breeds.

They show a special kind of loyalty to their true loved ones. Loyalty is coming when you call them, sitting on your lap, and the small glances they give you when they're trotting beside you to make sure you're still there. Loyalty is looking after you as much as you look after them, alerting you to danger, and barking or jumping in if you need help. They might be overly friendly, but they are faithful to you, first and foremost.

Gazers

When we gaze at our human babies, their oxytocin, or feel-good hormone, levels rise, and when they gaze back at us, our oxytocin levels rise too (and then theirs again, and then ours again, and on and on). It's an all-around love fest, a mutual gazing feedback loop that strengthens the bond between us. Well, we now know that dogs are officially our fur babies! According to *Science Magazine*, a new study shows that specific dog breeds (such as Labs and goldens) also take part in this oxytocin-releasing love fest with us. Dogs and humans both experience an increase in oxytocin when we gaze into each other's eyes. Now, it is a possibility that their fond feelings for us have something to do with the fact that they see us as playtime partners and treat givers. Perhaps, when they are gazing at us, what they're really thinking about is a peanut butter Kong, but that's okay. Isn't that still love? Whatever it is, we'll take it!

Loving Bond

Golden retrievers and their humans can form a bond that transcends all other relationships as they build trust and develop a loyal partnership. It feels incredible to walk with your golden trotting at your side, to be awoken in the morning by your golden's kisses, and to feel your golden's calm, caring presence when you are in need of a little comfort. You want to make your pup happy, and they want to do the same for you. They are our gorgeous furry friends, our protectors, our adventure buddies, our clumsy clowns, our kind and empathetic listeners, our joyful and exuberant playmates, and our loving and affectionate companions. They are our goldens.

Black Cat Golden Retriever Trope

Did you know that writers have adopted the golden as shorthand for a particular type of character often found in rom-coms? The "black cat golden retriever trope" is a common dynamic in books, movies, and other media in which two characters with contrasting personalities build a friendship or a romance with one another. Whereas the golden retriever in the relationship is friendly, social, open, and loyal, the black cat is aloof, mysterious, and independent with a deep desire to form a connection. The narrative device of the story hinges on the way their extreme differences ultimately bring the two unlikely mates together. The golden teaches the black cat how to be more open, outward, and trusting, and the black cat helps the golden retriever get in touch with their deep inner self. Examples include Emma and Mr. Knightley in Jane Austen's *Emma*, Sabrina and Linus in *Sabrina* with Audrey Hepburn, Harry and Sally in *When Harry Met Sally*, and many others in contemporary romance books.

Finding the Perfect Name for Your Golden Retriever

Looking for the right name to suit your pup's unique personality? Here's a list to help inspire you:

Abbie	Biscuit	Cody	Freya
Ace	Blanche	Cookie	George
Amber	Bowie	Cooper	Ginger
Apollo	Brady	Daisy	Gracie
Archie	Brie	Dakota	Gunnar
Aspen	Bruno	Danny	Gus
Autumn	Bud/Buddy	Diana	Hank
Bailey	Butter	Dixie	Harley
Beans	Callie	Donna	Harper
Bear	Champ	Dorothy/Dot	Harris
Beau	Charlie	Duke	Harry
Bella	Chase	Elio	Hazel
Benny	Chip	Ella	Henry
Betty	Chloe	Ellie	Honey
Billie	Clover	Elvis	Hudson
Birdie	Coco	Finn	Hunter

Indie
Ivy
Izzy
Jack
June
Juno
Kate
Kiki
Lady
Leo
Liberty
Lily
Lincoln
Lola
Lottie
Louie
Luca
Lucy
Luna
Mabel
Mac
Maggie
Maple
Margot
Maverick
Max
Mia
Millie
Milo
Mochi
Molly
Mozart
Muffin
Murphy
Murray
Nala
Nelly
Nelson
Nova
Oakley
Odie
Olive/Oliver
Opal
Oscar
Otto
Pancho
Peanut
Pearl
Penny
Pepper
Phoebe
Phoenix
Piper
Poppy
Prince
Pumpkin
Ranger
Ray
Riley
River
Rocky
Rookie
Rose/Rosie
Roxy
Ruby
Rudy
Sadie
Sage
Sam
Sandy
Scout
Sebastian
Simba
Sky
Sophia/Sophie
Stella
Sugar
Summer
Sunny
Taylor
Teddy
Thor
Toffee
Tucker
Tyler
Uma
Victor
Violet
Waffles
Walter
Willie
Willow
Winnie
Winston
Zoe

Taking Care of Your Golden Retriever

Health Considerations

Golden retrievers are prone to a variety of health issues such as hip or elbow dysplasia, eye problems, heart disease, and cancer. If purchasing your dog from a breeder, make sure they have screened for some of these conditions. Be sure to check with AKC to ensure you are working with a responsible breeder who has the golden retriever's health, behavior, and stability in mind.

Recommended Health Tests from the National Breed Club

- Hip Evaluation
- Neuronal Ceroid Lipofuscinosis 5 (Golden Retriever) (NCL, NCL5) - DNA Test
- Elbow Evaluation
- Cardiac Exam
- Ophthalmologist Evaluation

Breed Information from the AKC

akc.org/dog-breeds/golden-retriever

The Official Breed Club Health Statement

cdn.akc.org/Marketplace/Health-Statement/Golden-Retriever.pdf

Also visit Morris Animal Foundation, a global leader in animal health studies: "The Golden Retriever Lifetime Study is one of the largest, most comprehensive prospective canine health studies in the United States. The Study's purpose is to identify the nutritional, environmental, lifestyle and genetic risk factors for cancer and other diseases in dogs. Each year, with the help of veterinarians and dog owners, the Foundation collects health, environmental and behavioral data on 3,000+ enrolled golden retrievers."

For more information:

morrisanimalfoundation.org/golden-retriever-lifetime-study

Grooming

- Most of the time, a weekly brushing will do, but during the heavy shedding seasons, you'll want to brush your pup daily to remove some of the excess fur before it ends up on your rugs and furniture.
- Bathe your golden occasionally to keep them clean, more frequently during shedding seasons. Trim their nails regularly.

Exercise

- Golden retrievers require a lot of exercise, as do most sporting dogs, to keep them physically and mentally stimulated and prevent them from chewing your pillows and getting into trouble. A daily hike, run, or walk will do, and agility and obedience training will keep them sharp. They love to swim and are usually always up for fetch in the lake.
- Because goldens sometimes have joint issues in their elbows and hips, be sure all strenuous exercise is cleared with the vet.

Training

- It's important to start socializing and training your golden puppy early to get them used to different situations and to help them grow into a well-behaved adult. Join a socialization and training puppy class in your area.
- Golden retrievers are easy to train, intelligent, and eager to please, which makes obedience training a lot of fun and strengthens the bond between you.

Nutrition

- Golden retrievers require a well-balanced diet with high-quality proteins, fats, carbohydrates, vitamins, and minerals. Consider their calorie intake and monitor their weight, because they are prone to obesity, which can lead to other health issues.
- They should be given treats in moderation.
- Avoid table scraps when possible.
- Make sure all ingredients are dog safe, and always check with your vet with any questions about your pup's diet.

Golden Resources

The AKC Marketplace website offers resources for purchasing Labrador retriever puppies from a breeder. According to AKC, "AKC Marketplace is the only site to exclusively list 100% AKC puppies from AKC-Registered litters and the breeders who have cared for and raised these puppies are required to follow rules and regulations established by the AKC."

marketplace.akc.org/puppies/golden-retriever

Consider donating to the Golden Retriever Foundation to support their mission. They set out to rescue, foster, and promote the rehabilitation and placement of displaced golden retrievers into permanent homes, research diseases and genetic disorders that afflict them, and promote education about them.

goldenretrieverfoundation.org

Acknowledgments

I would like to thank my editor, Nicole James, for her vision and enthusiasm, as well as Sarah O'Connor and the whole team at Quarto for helping to bring this series of books about dogs to life. Thanks to my friends and readers of my work over the years, fellow artists in the Cut and Paste ARIM (Artist Residency in Motherhood), my writing teachers at Sarah Lawrence College, Tufts, and Friends School. Thank you to my close friends who have been there, always, supporting my writing. You know who you are. Thanks to my childhood dog, Sparky, and to my sweet and silly Sato dog, Cali, who makes us laugh and brings us endless joy and love. Thank you to the hard-working volunteers at Heaven Can Wait Rescue - Northstar Dogs for Adoption for bringing Cali to us. Finally, I would like to thank my family: my parents Jan and Michael, my sister Rachel, and my nieces, aunts, uncles, cousins, and in-laws. I'm incredibly grateful to my husband, Kevin, for his kindness, love, and support, and to my incredible daughters, Nora and Rosie, who will always have my heart.

About the Author

Sara Weiss holds an MFA from Sarah Lawrence College. She is the author of *A Frenchie Life*, *A Labrador Life*, and *The Totally Awesome World of Caitlin Clark*. Her writing has appeared in journals and magazines such as *Literary Mama*, *Mutha*, *Lilith*, *Waterwheel Review*, *Bustle*, and *Brain Child*, among others. She has written audio scripts for *Good Night Stories for Rebel Girls* and works as a college writing consultant. She lives in the Hudson Valley with her husband, two daughters, and their little Sato rescue dog Cali.

Who Can Have Just One Dog?

With so many breeds to love, collect and enjoy all the companion titles celebrating our favorite friends:

A Frenchie Life

What to Know and Love about the French Bulldog

ISBN: 978-1-57715-503-4

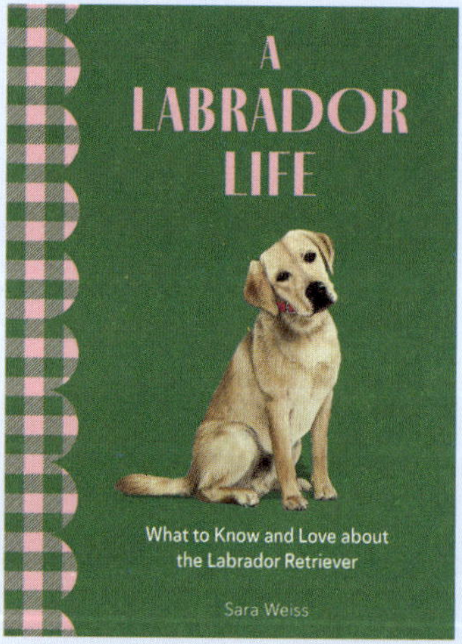

A Labrador Life

What to Know and Love about the Labrador Retriever

ISBN: 978-1-57715-504-1